Campbell's
CONDENSED SOUP

PARIS INTERNATIONAL EXPOSITION 1900

BACK LABEL
RECIPES
and more!

This edition is a revised and enlarged version of the soft-cover *Campbell's Back Label Recipes and more!*

Campbell's Back Label Recipes and more! was produced by the Global Publishing division of Campbell Soup Company, Campbell Place, Camden, NJ 08103-1799.

Senior Managing Editor:	Pat Teberg
Assistant Editors:	Peg Romano, Ginny Gance, Joanne Fullan
Marketing Manager:	Michael Conway
Promotions Director:	Terrence Atkins
Public Relations Manager:	Mary Beth Kramer
Global Consumer Food Center:	Ann Dungan, Jane Freiman, Nancy Speth
Photography:	Campbell Creative Photography
	Peter Walters Photography/Chicago
	Sacco Productions Limited/Chicago
Photographers:	Michael Brennan, Tom Dwyer, Tom O'Connell, Peter Ross,
	Coleman Sellers, Peter Walters
Photo Stylists/Production:	Betty Karslake, Sue Schilling, Paula Walters, Lynn Wilson
Food Stylists:	Amy Andrews, Betty Barlow, Donna Coates, Teri Ernst,
	Lois Hlavac, Moisette McNerney, Judy Mentzer,
	Lee Mooney, Gail O'Donnell, Carol Parik, Patricia Ward

Designed and published by Meredith Custom Publishing, 1912 Grand Avenue, Des Moines, IA 50309-3379.
Printed in Hong Kong.

Pictured on the front cover: One-Dish Chicken and Stuffing Bake *(page 16)*.

Preparation and Cooking Times: Every recipe was developed and tested in Campbell's Global Consumer Food Center by professional home economists. Use "Chill Time," "Cook Time," "Cool Time," "Marinating Time," "Prep Time" and/or "Stand Time" given with each recipe as guides. The preparation times are based on the approximate amount of time required to assemble the recipes *before* baking or cooking. These times include preparation steps, such as chopping; mixing; cooking rice, pasta, vegetables; etc. The fact that some preparation steps can be done simultaneously or during cooking is taken into account. The cook times are based on the minimum amount of time required to cook, bake or broil the food in the recipes.

Campbell's

BACK LABEL RECIPES
AND MORE!

SIMPLY DELICIOUS SUPPERS

Easy Chicken and Pasta, right (page 6)
and Creamy Chicken and Mushrooms, left (page 7).

EASY CHICKEN AND PASTA

1 tbsp. vegetable oil
1 lb. skinless, boneless chicken breasts,
    cut up
1 can (10¾ oz.) CAMPBELL'S condensed
    Cream of Chicken Soup
½ cup water
1 bag (about 16 oz.) frozen seasoned pasta
    and vegetable combination

1 In skillet over medium-high heat, heat oil. Cook chicken until browned, stirring often. Set chicken aside.

2 Add soup, water and vegetable combination. Heat to a boil. Return chicken to pan. Cover and cook over low heat 5 min. or until chicken is done, stirring occasionally.

Makes 4 servings
Prep Time: 5 min.
Cook Time: 20 min.

TOMATO-TOPPED CHICKEN AND STUFFING

5 cups PEPPERIDGE FARM Cubed Herb
    Seasoned Stuffing
2 tbsp. margarine, melted
1 cup boiling water
6 skinless, boneless chicken breast halves
1 can (10¾ oz.) CAMPBELL'S condensed
    Cream of Chicken Soup
⅓ cup milk
1 medium tomato, cut into 6 slices

1 Crush *1 cup* stuffing and mix with margarine. Set aside.

2 Lightly mix remaining stuffing and water. Spoon into 3-qt. shallow baking dish. Arrange chicken over stuffing.

3 Mix soup and milk. Spoon over chicken. Top with tomato. Sprinkle reserved stuffing mixture over tomato.

4 Bake at 400°F. 30 min. or until chicken is done.

Makes 6 servings
Prep Time: 15 min.
Cook Time: 30 min.

CREAMY CHICKEN AND MUSHROOMS

2 tbsp. margarine

4 skinless, boneless chicken breast halves

1½ cups sliced mushrooms

1 small onion, sliced

⅛ tsp. garlic powder

1 can (10¾ oz.) CAMPBELL'S condensed Cream of Mushroom Soup

½ cup milk

2 tbsp. dry sherry (optional)

⅛ tsp. pepper

4 cups hot cooked bow tie macaroni *or* medium egg noodles

1 In skillet over medium-high heat, heat *half* the margarine. Cook chicken 10 min. or until browned. Set chicken aside.

2 Add remaining margarine. Add mushrooms, onion and garlic powder. Cook over medium heat until tender.

3 Add soup, milk, sherry and pepper. Heat to a boil. Return chicken to pan. Cover and cook over low heat 5 min. or until chicken is done. Serve with noodles. If desired, garnish with *fresh rosemary.*

Makes 4 servings
Prep Time: 10 min.
Cook Time: 25 min.

Substitute 2 cans (5 oz. *each*) SWANSON Premium Chunk White *or* Chunk Chicken for cubed cooked chicken.

CHICKEN NOODLE PARMESAN

1 can (10¾ oz.) CAMPBELL'S condensed Cream of Chicken Soup

½ cup milk

⅛ tsp. pepper

⅓ cup grated Parmesan cheese

2 cups cubed cooked chicken

3 cups cooked medium egg noodles

In saucepan mix soup, milk, pepper, cheese, chicken and noodles. Over medium heat, heat through, stirring occasionally.

Makes 4 servings
Prep Time: 15 min.
Cook Time: 10 min.

LEMON ASPARAGUS CHICKEN

1 tbsp. vegetable oil

4 skinless, boneless chicken breast halves

1 can (10¾ oz.) CAMPBELL'S condensed Cream of Asparagus Soup

¼ cup milk

1 tbsp. lemon juice

⅛ tsp. pepper

1 In skillet over medium-high heat, heat oil. Cook chicken 10 min. or until browned. Set chicken aside. Pour off fat.

2 Add soup, milk, lemon juice and pepper. Heat to a boil. Return chicken to pan. Cover and cook over low heat 5 min. or until chicken is done. If desired, serve over hot cooked *linguine*.

Makes 4 servings

Prep Time: 5 min.

Cook Time: 20 min.

When purchasing chicken, buy about ½ lb. bone-in chicken or ¼ lb. skinless, boneless chicken for each main-dish serving.

SKILLET HERB CHICKEN

2 tbsp. all-purpose flour

¼ tsp. ground sage

¼ tsp. dried thyme leaves, crushed

4 skinless, boneless chicken breast halves

2 tbsp. margarine

1 can (10¾ oz.) CAMPBELL'S condensed Cream of Celery Soup

½ cup water

4 cups hot cooked rice

1 Mix flour, sage and thyme on plate. Coat chicken with flour mixture.

2 In skillet over medium heat, heat margarine. Cook chicken 15 min. or until chicken is done. Remove and keep warm.

3 Add soup and water. Heat through. Serve with chicken and rice.

Makes 4 servings

Prep Time: 10 min.

Cook Time: 20 min.

EASY CHICKEN PAPRIKASH

1 tbsp. margarine

4 skinless, boneless chicken breast halves

1 can (10¾ oz.) CAMPBELL'S condensed Cream of Mushroom Soup

2 tsp. paprika

⅛ tsp. ground red pepper

⅓ cup sour cream

4 cups hot cooked spaetzle *or* medium egg noodles

1 In skillet over medium-high heat, heat margarine. Cook chicken 10 min. or until browned. Set chicken aside.

2 Add soup, paprika and pepper. Heat to a boil. Return chicken to pan. Cover and cook over low heat 5 min. or until chicken is done.

3 Stir in sour cream. Heat through. Serve with spaetzle. If desired, garnish with *cherry tomatoes* and *fresh parsley*.

Makes 4 servings
Prep Time: 5 min.
Cook Time: 25 min.

SOUTHERN-STYLE BARBECUED CHICKEN

1 can (10¾ oz.) CAMPBELL'S condensed Tomato Soup

2 tbsp. honey

1 tsp. dry mustard

½ tsp. onion powder

4 chicken breast halves, skinned

1 Mix soup, honey, mustard and onion powder.

2 Broil chicken 6" from heat 30 min. or until chicken is done, turning and brushing often with soup mixture.

Makes 4 servings
Prep Time: 10 min.
Cook Time: 30 min.

Chicken Crunch

1 can (10¾ oz.) CAMPBELL'S condensed
    Cream of Chicken Soup
½ cup milk
4 skinless, boneless chicken breast halves
2 tbsp. all-purpose flour
1½ cups PEPPERIDGE FARM Herb Seasoned
    Stuffing, finely crushed
2 tbsp. margarine, melted

1 Mix ⅓ *cup* soup and ¼ *cup* milk in dish. Lightly coat chicken with flour. Dip into soup mixture. Coat with stuffing.

2 Place chicken on baking sheet. Drizzle with margarine. Bake at 400°F. 20 min. or until chicken is done.

3 In saucepan mix remaining soup and remaining milk. Heat through. Serve with chicken. If desired, garnish with *fresh rosemary*.

Makes 4 servings
Prep Time: 15 min.
Cook Time: 20 min.

Chicken Supreme

1 tbsp. vegetable oil
4 skinless, boneless chicken breast halves
1 can (10¾ oz.) CAMPBELL'S condensed
    Cream of Celery Soup
½ cup milk
⅛ tsp. pepper
4 cups hot cooked rice

1 In skillet over medium-high heat, heat oil. Cook chicken 10 min. or until browned. Set chicken aside. Pour off fat.

2 Add soup, milk and pepper. Heat to a boil. Return chicken to pan. Cover and cook over low heat 5 min. or until chicken is done. Serve with rice.

Makes 4 servings
Prep Time: 5 min.
Cook Time: 20 min.

CHICKEN BROCCOLI DIVAN

1 lb. broccoli, cut into spears, cooked and drained
1½ cups cubed cooked chicken
1 can (10¾ oz.) CAMPBELL'S condensed Cream of Broccoli Soup
⅓ cup milk
½ cup shredded Cheddar cheese
2 tbsp. dry bread crumbs
1 tbsp. margarine, melted

1 In 9" pie plate or 2-qt. shallow baking dish arrange broccoli and chicken. Mix soup and milk. Pour over broccoli and chicken.
2 Sprinkle cheese and bread crumbs mixed with margarine over top. Bake at 450°F. 20 min. or until hot.

Makes 4 servings
Prep Time: 15 min.
Cook Time: 20 min.

EASY CHICKEN AND BISCUITS

- **1 can (10¾ oz.) CAMPBELL'S condensed Cream of Celery Soup**
- **1 can (10¾ oz.) CAMPBELL'S condensed Cream of Potato Soup**
- **1 cup milk**
- **¼ tsp. dried thyme leaves, crushed**
- **¼ tsp. pepper**
- **4 cups cooked cut-up vegetables***
- **2 cups cubed cooked chicken**
- **1 pkg. (7½ or 10 oz.) refrigerated butter-milk biscuits**

1 In 3-qt. shallow baking dish mix soups, milk, thyme, pepper, vegetables and chicken.

2 Bake at 400°F. 15 min. or until hot.

3 Stir. Arrange biscuits over chicken mixture. Bake 15 min. or until biscuits are golden.

Makes 5 servings
Prep Time: 15 min.
Cook Time: 30 min.

*Use a combination of broccoli flowerets, cauliflower flowerets and carrots.

CHICKEN AND MUSHROOMS DIJON

2 tbsp. margarine

4 skinless, boneless chicken breast halves

1½ cups broccoli flowerets

1½ cups sliced mushrooms

1 can (10¾ oz.) CAMPBELL'S condensed Cream of Chicken & Broccoli Soup

¼ cup milk

2 tbsp. Dijon-style mustard

4 cups hot cooked medium egg noodles

1 In skillet over medium-high heat, heat *half* the margarine. Cook chicken 10 min. or until browned. Set chicken aside.

2 Add remaining margarine. Add broccoli and mushrooms. Cook over medium heat until tender.

3 Add soup, milk and mustard. Heat to a boil. Return chicken to pan. Cover and cook over low heat 5 min. or until chicken is done. Serve with noodles.

Makes 4 servings
Prep Time: 10 min.
Cook Time: 25 min.

ONE-DISH CHICKEN AND STUFFING BAKE *(pictured on cover)*

4 cups PEPPERIDGE FARM Herb Seasoned Stuffing

1¼ cups boiling water

4 tbsp. margarine, melted*

4 to 6 skinless, boneless chicken breast halves

Paprika

1 can (10¾ oz.) CAMPBELL'S condensed Cream of Mushroom Soup

⅓ cup milk

1 tbsp. chopped fresh parsley

*For a lower fat stuffing, reduce margarine to 1 tbsp.

1 Mix stuffing, water and margarine.

2 Spoon stuffing across center of 3-qt. shallow baking dish. Arrange chicken on each side of stuffing. Sprinkle chicken with paprika.

3 Mix soup, milk and parsley. Pour over chicken.

4 Cover and bake at 400°F. 30 min. or until chicken is no longer pink.

Makes 4 to 6 servings
Prep Time: 10 min.
Cook Time: 30 min.

SAUTÉED CHICKEN BREASTS

2 tbsp. all-purpose flour

⅛ tsp. pepper

4 skinless, boneless chicken breast halves

2 tbsp. vegetable oil

1 can (11⅛ oz.) CAMPBELL'S condensed Italian Tomato Soup

½ cup water

1 Mix flour and pepper on plate. Coat chicken with flour mixture.

2 In skillet over medium-high heat, heat oil. Cook chicken 10 min. or until browned. Set chicken aside. Pour off fat.

3 Add soup and water. Heat to a boil. Return chicken to pan. Cover and cook over low heat 5 min. or until chicken is done.

Makes 4 servings
Prep Time: 10 min.
Cook Time: 20 min.

Substitute 2 cans (5 oz. _each_) SWANSON Premium Chunk White _or_ Chunk Chicken for chopped cooked chicken.

SOUPER ENCHILADAS

1 can (10¾ oz.) CAMPBELL'S condensed Cream of Chicken Soup

½ cup sour cream

1 tbsp. margarine

1 medium onion, chopped

1 tsp. chili powder

2 cups chopped cooked chicken

1 can (about 4 oz.) chopped green chilies

8 flour tortillas (8")

1 cup shredded Cheddar cheese

1 Mix soup and sour cream.

2 In saucepan over medium heat, heat margarine. Cook onion and chili powder until tender. Add chicken, chilies and _2 tbsp._ soup mixture.

3 Spread _½ cup_ soup mixture in 2-qt. shallow baking dish. Spoon about _¼ cup_ chicken mixture on each tortilla. Roll tortilla around filling and place seam-side down in baking dish.

4 Spread remaining soup mixture over enchiladas. Sprinkle cheese over top. Bake at 350°F. 25 min. or until hot.

Makes 4 servings
Prep Time: 25 min.
Cook Time: 25 min.

CHICKEN RICE SKILLET

1 tbsp. vegetable oil

2 lb. chicken parts

1 can (10½ oz.) CAMPBELL'S condensed Chicken Broth

¼ tsp. garlic powder

¼ tsp. hot pepper sauce (optional)

1 large green pepper, chopped

¾ cup drained cut-up canned tomatoes

⅔ cup uncooked regular long-grain rice

1 In skillet over medium-high heat, heat oil. Cook chicken 10 min. or until browned. Set chicken aside. Pour off fat.

2 Add broth, garlic powder, hot pepper sauce, green pepper, tomatoes and rice. Heat to a boil. Return chicken to pan. Cover and cook over low heat 30 min. or until chicken and rice are done.

Makes 4 servings

Prep Time: 10 min.

Cook Time: 45 min.

TOMATO CHICKEN STIR-FRY

2 tbsp. vegetable oil

**1 lb. skinless, boneless chicken breasts
cut into strips**

3 cups cut-up vegetables*

½ tsp. ground ginger

¼ tsp. garlic powder

**1 can (10¾ oz.) CAMPBELL'S condensed
Tomato Soup**

2 tbsp. soy sauce

1 tbsp. vinegar

4 cups hot cooked rice

*Use a combination of broccoli flowerets, cauliflower
flowerets and carrots.

1 In skillet over medium-high heat, heat *half* the oil.
Stir-fry chicken in 2 batches until browned. Set
chicken aside.

2 Add remaining oil. Add vegetables, ginger and garlic
powder. Stir-fry over medium heat until tender-crisp.

3 Add soup, soy and vinegar. Heat to a boil. Return
chicken to pan. Heat through. Serve over rice.

Makes 4 servings
Prep Time: 15 min.
Cook Time: 25 min.

Pasta Primavera

2 tbsp. cornstarch
1 can (10½ oz.) CAMPBELL'S condensed
   Chicken Broth
½ cup water
1 tsp. dried basil leaves, crushed
¼ tsp. garlic powder
2 cups broccoli flowerets
2 medium carrots, sliced
1 medium onion, cut into wedges
1 medium tomato, diced
4 cups hot cooked thin spaghetti
   Grated Parmesan cheese

1 Mix cornstarch and ¾ *cup* broth until smooth. Set aside.

2 In saucepan mix remaining broth, water, basil, garlic powder, broccoli, carrots and onion. Over medium-high heat, heat to a boil. Cover and cook over low heat 5 min. or until vegetables are tender.

3 Stir cornstarch mixture and add. Cook until mixture boils and thickens, stirring constantly. Stir in tomato. Toss with spaghetti. Serve with cheese.

Makes 4 servings
Prep Time: 15 min.
Cook Time: 15 min.

Oriental Chicken Skillet

1 tbsp. vegetable oil
4 skinless, boneless chicken breast halves
1 can (10¾ oz.) CAMPBELL'S condensed
   Cream of Chicken Soup
⅓ cup water
1 tbsp. soy sauce
¼ tsp. ground ginger
1 pkg. (about 10 oz.) frozen cut
   green beans
2 green onions, cut into 1" pieces
4 cups hot cooked rice

1 In skillet over medium-high heat, heat oil. Cook chicken 10 min. or until browned. Set chicken aside. Pour off fat.

2 Add soup, water, soy, ginger, beans and onions. Heat to a boil. Return chicken to pan. Cover and cook over low heat 5 min. or until chicken is done. Serve with rice.

Makes 4 servings
Prep Time: 10 min.
Cook Time: 20 min.

BEST-EVER MEAT LOAF

1 **can (11⅛ oz.) CAMPBELL'S condensed Italian Tomato Soup**
2 **lb. ground beef**
1 **pouch CAMPBELL'S Dry Onion Soup and Recipe Mix**
½ **cup dry bread crumbs**
1 **egg, beaten**
¼ **cup water**

1 Mix ½ *cup* Italian tomato soup, beef, soup mix, bread crumbs and egg *thoroughly*. In baking pan shape *firmly* into 8" x 4" loaf.

2 Bake at 350°F. 1¼ hr. or until meat loaf is done (160°F.).

3 In saucepan mix *2 tbsp.* drippings, remaining soup and water. Heat through. Serve with meat loaf. If desired, garnish with *baby corn, zucchini, tomatoes* and *fresh sage.*

Makes 8 servings
Prep Time: 10 min.
Cook Time: 1 hr. 20 min.

TERIYAKI BEEF KABOBS

2 **tbsp. cornstarch**
1 **can (10½ oz.) CAMPBELL'S condensed Beef Broth**
½ **cup water**
2 **tbsp. soy sauce**
1 **tbsp. packed brown sugar**
¼ **tsp. garlic powder**
¼ **tsp. ground ginger**
1 **lb. boneless beef sirloin steak, cut into 1" cubes**
12 **medium mushrooms**
2 **medium red onions, each cut into 6 wedges**
4 **cherry tomatoes**
4 **cups hot cooked rice**

1 In saucepan mix cornstarch, broth, water, soy, sugar, garlic powder and ginger until smooth. Over medium heat, cook until mixture boils and thickens, stirring constantly.

2 On 4 long skewers, thread beef, mushrooms and onions alternately.

3 Grill kabobs on lightly oiled grill rack over medium-hot coals to desired doneness (20 min. for medium), turning and brushing often with broth mixture. Place 1 tomato on end of each skewer.

4 Heat remaining broth mixture to a boil. Serve with kabobs and rice.

Makes 4 servings
Prep Time: 15 min.
Cook Time: 20 min.

Skillet Mac 'n' Beef

1 lb. ground beef
1 medium onion, chopped
1 can (10¾ oz.) CAMPBELL'S condensed
    Cream of Celery Soup
¼ cup ketchup
1 tbsp. Worcestershire sauce
2 cups cooked corkscrew macaroni

1 In skillet over medium-high heat, cook beef and onion until beef is browned, stirring to separate meat. Pour off fat.

2 Add soup, ketchup, Worcestershire and macaroni. Over low heat, heat through. If desired, garnish with *cherry tomatoes* and *fresh basil*.

Makes 4 servings
Prep Time: 10 min.
Cook Time: 15 min.

Savory Pot Roast

2 tbsp. vegetable oil
3½- to 4-lb. boneless beef bottom round *or*
    chuck pot roast
1 can (10¾ oz.) CAMPBELL'S condensed
    Cream of Mushroom Soup
1¼ cups water
1 pouch CAMPBELL'S Dry Onion Soup
    and Recipe Mix
6 medium potatoes, cut into quarters
6 medium carrots, cut into 2" pieces
2 tbsp. all-purpose flour

1 In Dutch oven over medium-high heat, heat oil. Cook roast until browned. Pour off fat.

2 Add mushroom soup, *1 cup* water and soup mix. Heat to a boil. Cover and cook over low heat 1½ hr.

3 Add potatoes and carrots. Cover and cook 1 hr. or until roast is done, stirring occasionally.

4 Remove roast and vegetables. Mix flour and remaining water until smooth. Add gradually to soup mixture. Over medium heat, cook until mixture boils and thickens, stirring constantly. Serve with roast and vegetables.

Makes 8 servings
Prep Time: 5 min.
Cook Time: 2 hr. 50 min.

BEEF AND MUSHROOMS DIJON

1 lb. boneless beef sirloin steak, ¾" thick
2 tbsp. vegetable oil
2 cups sliced mushrooms
1 medium onion, sliced
1 can (10¾ oz.) CAMPBELL'S condensed
   Cream of Mushroom Soup
½ cup water
2 tbsp. Dijon-style mustard
4 cups hot cooked rice

1 Slice beef into very thin strips.

2 In skillet over medium-high heat, heat *half* the oil. Cook beef in 2 batches until browned, stirring often. Set beef aside.

3 Add remaining oil. Add mushrooms and onion. Cook over medium heat until tender.

4 Add soup, water and mustard. Heat to a boil. Return beef to pan. Heat through. Serve over rice. If desired, garnish with *fresh chives*.

Makes 4 servings
Prep Time: 15 min.
Cook Time: 25 min.

SIMPLE SALISBURY STEAK

1 can (10¾ oz.) CAMPBELL'S condensed
   Cream of Mushroom Soup
1 lb. ground beef
⅓ cup dry bread crumbs
1 small onion, finely chopped
1 egg, beaten
1 tbsp. vegetable oil
1½ cups sliced mushrooms

1 Mix ¼ *cup* soup, beef, bread crumbs, onion and egg *thoroughly*. Shape *firmly* into 4 patties, ½" thick.

2 In skillet over medium-high heat, heat oil. Cook patties until browned. Set patties aside. Pour off fat.

3 Add remaining soup and mushrooms. Heat to a boil. Return patties to pan. Cover and cook over low heat 20 min. or until patties are done (160°F.).

Makes 4 servings
Prep Time: 15 min.
Cook Time: 30 min.

EASY PARTY LASAGNA

**1 can (10¾ oz.) CAMPBELL'S condensed
    Cream of Mushroom Soup**
2 cups shredded mozzarella cheese
¼ cup milk
1 lb. ground beef
**1 can (11⅛ oz.) CAMPBELL'S condensed
    Italian Tomato Soup**
1 cup water
6 *dry* lasagna noodles

1 Mix mushroom soup, *½ cup* cheese and milk.
   Set aside.
2 In skillet over medium-high heat, cook beef until
   browned, stirring to separate meat. Pour off fat. Stir
   in Italian tomato soup and water. Heat through.

3 In 2-qt. shallow baking dish spoon *half* the meat
   mixture. Top with *3* lasagna noodles and mushroom
   soup mixture. Top with remaining *3* lasagna noodles
   and remaining meat mixture. Cover.
4 Bake at 400°F. 40 min. or until hot. Uncover.
   Sprinkle remaining cheese over top. Bake 10 min. or
   until cheese is melted. Let stand 10 min. If desired,
   garnish with *tomato, fresh basil, bay leaves* and *finely
   shredded Parmesan cheese.*

Makes 8 servings
Prep Time: 20 min.
Cook Time: 50 min.
Stand Time: 10 min.

ITALIAN GRILLED BEEF

**1 can (11⅛ oz.) CAMPBELL'S condensed
    Italian Tomato Soup**
**½ cup prepared Italian
    salad dressing**
1½ lb. boneless beef sirloin steak, ¾" thick

1 Mix soup and dressing.
2 Grill steak on lightly oiled grill rack over medium-
   hot coals to desired doneness (15 min. for medium),
   turning once and brushing often with soup mixture.
3 Heat remaining soup mixture to a boil. Serve with
   steak.

Makes 6 servings
Prep Time: 5 min.
Cook Time: 15 min.

PORK CHOP SKILLET DINNER

1 tbsp. olive oil

4 pork shoulder chops, ¾" thick

1 medium onion, chopped

1 cup uncooked regular long-grain rice

1 can (10½ oz.) CAMPBELL'S condensed Chicken Broth

1 cup orange juice

3 tbsp. chopped fresh parsley

4 orange slices, halved

1 In skillet over medium-high heat, heat oil. Cook chops 10 min. or until browned. Set chops aside.

2 Add onion and rice. Cook over medium heat until rice is browned, stirring constantly. Stir in broth, orange juice and *2 tbsp.* parsley. Heat to a boil. Return chops to pan. Cover and cook over low heat 20 min. or until chops and rice are done.

3 Top with orange slices and sprinkle with remaining parsley. If desired, garnish with additional *fresh parsley.*

Makes 4 servings

Prep Time: 10 min.

Cook Time: 40 min.

Substitute 2 cups cooked elbow macaroni (about 1 cup dry) for the corkscrew macaroni.

BEEFY MACARONI SKILLET

1 lb. ground beef

1 medium onion, chopped

1 can (10¾ oz.) CAMPBELL'S condensed Tomato Soup

¼ cup water

1 tbsp. Worcestershire sauce

½ cup shredded Cheddar cheese

2 cups cooked corkscrew macaroni

1 In skillet over medium-high heat, cook beef and onion until beef is browned, stirring to separate meat. Pour off fat.

2 Add soup, water, Worcestershire, cheese and macaroni. Over low heat, heat through.

Makes 4 servings

Prep Time: 10 min.

Cook Time: 15 min.

GLORIFIED PORK CHOPS

2 tbsp. vegetable oil
6 pork chops, ½" thick
1 medium onion, sliced
1 can (10¾ oz.) CAMPBELL'S condensed
    Cream of Celery Soup
¼ cup water

1 In skillet over medium-high heat, heat *half* the oil.
   Cook chops in 2 batches 10 min. or until browned.
   Set chops aside.

2 Add remaining oil. Add onion. Cook over medium
   heat until tender. Pour off fat.
3 Add soup and water. Heat to a boil. Return chops to
   pan. Cover and cook over low heat 5 min. or until
   chops are done.

Makes 6 servings
Prep Time: 5 min.
Cook Time: 30 min.

VEGETABLE BEEF AND BISCUIT CASSEROLE

1½ lb. ground beef
1 can (10¾ oz.) CAMPBELL'S condensed
    Tomato Soup
1 can (10¾ oz.) CAMPBELL'S condensed
    Golden Corn Soup
¾ cup water
1 tbsp. Worcestershire sauce
1 can (15 oz.) mixed vegetables, drained
1 pkg. (7½ or 10 oz.) refrigerated butter-
    milk biscuits
½ cup shredded Cheddar cheese

1 In skillet over medium-high heat, cook beef until
   browned, stirring to separate meat. Pour off fat.
2 Add soups, water, Worcestershire and vegetables.
   Spoon into 3-qt. shallow baking dish. Bake at 400°F.
   10 min. or until hot.
3 Stir. Arrange biscuits over beef mixture. Top with
   cheese. Bake 15 min. or until biscuits are golden.

Makes 6 servings
Prep Time: 15 min.
Cook Time: 25 min.

CAMPBELL'S CHUNKY SOUPS MAKE THE MEAL

CHICKEN AND RICE

1 can (19 oz.) CAMPBELL'S CHUNKY
   Old Fashioned Chicken Soup
1 cup uncooked instant rice

In saucepan over medium heat, heat soup to a boil. Stir in rice. Cover and set aside 5 min. Stir.

Makes 2 servings
Prep Time: 5 min.
Cook Time: 5 min.
Stand Time: 5 min.

QUICK BEEF AND BROCCOLI

1 can (19 oz.) CAMPBELL'S CHUNKY Pepper
   Steak Soup
1 tsp. soy sauce
¼ tsp. garlic powder
1 cup cooked broccoli flowerets
2 cups hot cooked rice

In saucepan mix soup, soy, garlic powder and broccoli. Over medium heat, heat through, stirring occasionally. Serve over rice.

Makes 2 servings
Prep Time: 15 min.
Cook Time: 5 min.

CHUNKY VEGETABLES AND MACARONI

1 can (19 oz.) CAMPBELL'S CHUNKY
   Vegetable Soup
¼ tsp. garlic powder
½ cup cooked cut green beans
1 tbsp. grated Parmesan cheese
1 cup cooked elbow macaroni

In saucepan mix soup, garlic powder, beans, cheese and macaroni. Over medium heat, heat through, stirring occasionally.

Makes 2 servings
Prep Time: 15 min.
Cook Time: 5 min.

ORIENTAL VEGETABLES AND BEEF

1 tbsp. vegetable oil
1 cup broccoli flowerets
1 can (19 oz.) CAMPBELL'S CHUNKY
   Old Fashioned Vegetable Beef Soup
1 tbsp. soy sauce
2 cups cooked rice

In saucepan over medium heat, heat oil. Cook broccoli until tender-crisp. Add soup, soy and rice. Heat through, stirring occasionally.

Makes 2 servings
Prep Time: 20 min
Cook Time: 10 min.

Chicken and Rice (top)
Quick Beef and Broccoli (bottom)

FOOLPROOF FAMILY SIZE RECIPES

CREAMY MUSHROOM BARLEY SOUP

- 2 tbsp. margarine
- 1 cup sliced mushrooms
- 1 medium onion, chopped
- ⅓ cup uncooked barley
- 1 can (26 oz.) CAMPBELL'S condensed
    Cream of Mushroom Soup
- 3 cups water
- ¼ tsp. dried thyme leaves, crushed
- ¼ tsp. pepper

1 In saucepan over medium heat, heat margarine. Cook mushrooms and onion until tender. Add barley. Cook until lightly browned, stirring constantly.

2 Add soup, water, thyme and pepper. Heat to a boil. Cover and cook over low heat 40 min. or until barley is done, stirring occasionally. If desired, garnish with *fresh thyme* and *sweet red pepper.*

Makes 6 servings
Prep Time: 10 min.
Cook Time: 50 min.

QUICK BARBECUED BEEF SANDWICHES

- 1 tbsp. vegetable oil
- 1 medium onion, chopped
- 1 can (26 oz.) CAMPBELL'S condensed
    Tomato Soup
- ¼ cup water
- 2 tbsp. packed brown sugar
- 2 tbsp. vinegar
- 1 tbsp. Worcestershire sauce
- 1½ lb. thinly sliced cooked roast beef
- 12 round sandwich *or* hamburger rolls,
    split and toasted

1 In Dutch oven over medium heat, heat oil. Cook onion until tender.

2 Add soup, water, sugar, vinegar and Worcestershire. Heat to a boil. Cook over low heat 5 min. Add beef. Heat through. Divide meat mixture among 12 roll halves. Top with remaining roll halves.

Makes 12 sandwiches
Prep Time: 10 min.
Cook Time: 20 min.

Creamy Mushroom Barley Soup (top)
Quick Barbecued Beef Sandwiches (bottom)

CAN-DO
SOUPS
& STEWS

Country Chicken Stew, left (page 43) and
Home-Style Beef Stew, right (page 42).

HOME-STYLE BEEF STEW

2 tbsp. all-purpose flour

⅛ tsp. pepper

1 lb. beef for stew, cut into 1" cubes

1 tbsp. vegetable oil

1 can (10½ oz.) CAMPBELL'S condensed Beef Broth

½ cup water

½ tsp. dried thyme leaves, crushed

1 bay leaf

3 medium carrots, cut into 1" pieces

2 medium potatoes, cut into quarters

1 Mix flour and pepper on plate. Coat beef with flour mixture.

2 In Dutch oven over medium-high heat, heat oil. Cook beef until browned, stirring often. Set beef aside. Pour off fat.

3 Add broth, water, thyme and bay leaf. Heat to a boil. Return beef to pan. Cover and cook over low heat 1½ hr.

4 Add carrots and potatoes. Cover and cook 30 min. or until beef is done. Discard bay leaf. If desired, garnish with *lemon peel, bay leaves* and *fresh thyme.*

Makes 4 servings

Prep Time: 10 min.

Cook Time: 2 hr. 15 min.

MEXICAN BEEF STEW

1½ lb. ground beef

1 large onion, chopped

¼ tsp. garlic powder

1 can (10¾ oz.) CAMPBELL'S condensed Tomato Soup

1 can (10½ oz.) CAMPBELL'S condensed Beef Broth

1 cup water

2 tbsp. chili powder

3 medium potatoes, cut into cubes

1 can (about 16 oz.) whole kernel corn, drained

Shredded Cheddar cheese

1 In saucepan over medium-high heat, cook beef, onion and garlic powder until beef is browned, stirring to separate meat. Pour off fat.

2 Add soup, broth, water, chili powder and potatoes. Heat to a boil. Cover and cook over low heat 15 min. or until potatoes are tender, stirring occasionally. Add corn. Heat through. Top with cheese.

Makes 6 servings

Prep Time: 15 min.

Cook Time: 30 min.

COUNTRY CHICKEN STEW

2 tbsp. margarine

1 medium onion, sliced

1 can (10¾ oz.) CAMPBELL'S condensed
   Cream of Chicken Soup

1 soup can water

½ tsp. dried oregano leaves, crushed

3 medium potatoes, cut into 1" pieces

2 medium carrots, sliced

1 cup frozen cut green beans

2 cups cubed cooked chicken

2 tbsp. chopped fresh parsley

2 slices bacon, cooked and crumbled

1 In skillet over medium heat, heat margarine. Cook onion until tender.

2 Add soup, water, oregano, potatoes and carrots. Heat to a boil. Cover and cook over low heat 15 min., stirring occasionally.

3 Add beans. Cover and cook 10 min. or until vegetables are tender, stirring occasionally. Add chicken, parsley and bacon. Heat through. If desired, garnish with *fresh parsley.*

Makes 4 servings
Prep Time: 15 min.
Cook Time: 40 min.

 Substitute 2 cans (5 oz. *each*) SWANSON Premium Chunk White *or* Chunk Chicken for cubed cooked chicken.

CHILI CON CARNE

1 lb. ground beef

1 medium onion, chopped

2 cans (11⅛ oz. *each*) CAMPBELL'S
   condensed Fiesta Tomato Soup

1 cup water

1 can (about 15 oz.) kidney beans, rinsed
   and drained
   Shredded Cheddar cheese

1 In skillet over medium-high heat, cook beef and onion until beef is browned, stirring to separate meat. Pour off fat.

2 Add soup, water and beans. Over low heat, heat through. Top with cheese.

Makes 5 servings
Prep Time: 5 min.
Cook Time: 10 min.

MAKE IT HEARTY

Here are five delicious ways to warm up your day or to make soup the centerpiece to lunch or dinner. Simply open your cabinet and add a few ingredients. It's that easy to make soup as *hearty* as you are hungry!

Pictured clockwise from top left: Hearty Beef Noodle Soup, Hearty Chicken with White and Wild Rice Soup and Hearty California Vegetable Soup.

MAKE IT HEARTY:	CAMPBELL'S Soup
Hearty Beef Noodle Soup	1 can (10¾ oz.) Beef Noodle Soup
Hearty Chicken with White and Wild Rice Soup	1 can (10½ oz.) Chicken with White & Wild Rice Soup
Hearty California Vegetable Soup	1 can (10¾ oz.) California-Style Vegetable Soup
Hearty Chicken Noodle Soup	1 can (10¾ oz.) Homestyle Chicken Noodle Soup
Hearty Minestrone Soup	1 can (10¾ oz.) Minestrone Soup

METHOD: In saucepan, combine soup, water and ADDITIONS.
Over medium heat, heat through, stirring often. Serves 2.

Water	Meat Addition	Vegetable Addition
1 soup can water	————	½ cup cooked mixed vegetables
1 soup can water	½ cup cubed cooked chicken	½ cup cooked peas
1 soup can water	————	1 cup cooked vegetable combination
1 soup can water	½ cup cubed cooked chicken	½ cup cooked mixed vegetables
1 soup can water	————	½ cup cooked cubed potato

CREAMY POTATO SOUP

1 tbsp. margarine
1 stalk celery, sliced
4 green onions, sliced
1 can (10½ oz.) CAMPBELL'S condensed Chicken Broth
½ cup water
⅛ tsp. pepper
3 medium potatoes, peeled and sliced ¼" thick
1½ cups milk

1 In saucepan over medium heat, heat margarine. Cook celery and onions until tender.

2 Add broth, water, pepper and potatoes. Heat to a boil. Cover and cook over low heat 15 min. or until potatoes are tender. Remove from heat.

3 In blender, place *half* the soup mixture and ¾ *cup* milk. Cover and blend until smooth. Repeat with remaining soup mixture and remaining milk. Return to pan. Over medium heat, heat through, stirring occasionally. If desired, garnish with *fresh parsley* and *fresh chives*.

Makes 5 servings
Prep Time: 15 min.
Cook Time: 30 min.

POTATO CORN CHOWDER

1 tbsp. margarine
1 stalk celery, chopped
1 medium onion, chopped
1 cup water
⅛ tsp. pepper
1 bay leaf
2 medium potatoes, cut into cubes
1 can (10¾ oz.) CAMPBELL'S condensed Golden Corn Soup
1 cup milk
4 slices bacon, cooked and crumbled (optional)

1 In saucepan over medium heat, heat margarine. Cook celery and onion until tender.

2 Add water, pepper, bay leaf and potatoes. Heat to a boil. Cover and cook over low heat 15 min. or until potatoes are tender.

3 Add soup, milk and bacon. Heat through, stirring occasionally. Discard bay leaf.

Makes 4 servings
Prep Time: 15 min.
Cook Time: 30 min.

MAKE IT HEARTY

Stir up some excitement at lunch or dinner with these souper-easy recipes.

With Campbell's soups, plus a few extra ingredients, you'll have even more ways

to make mealtime great!

Pictured clockwise from top left: Hearty Manhattan Clam Chowder, Hearty Turkey Noodle Soup and Hearty Vegetable Soup.

MAKE IT HEARTY:	CAMPBELL'S Soup
Hearty Manhattan Clam Chowder	1 can (10¾ oz.) Manhattan Clam Chowder
Hearty Turkey Noodle Soup	1 can (10½ oz.) Turkey Noodle Soup
Hearty Vegetable Soup	1 can (10¾ oz.) Homestyle Vegetable Soup
Hearty Chicken Vegetable Soup	1 can (10¾ oz.) Chicken Vegetable Soup
Hearty Creamy Chicken Noodle Soup	1 can (10¾ oz.) Creamy Chicken Noodle Soup

METHOD: In saucepan, combine soup, water *or* milk and ADDITIONS. Over medium heat, heat through, stirring often. Serves 2.

Water/Milk	Meat/Pasta Addition	Vegetable/Seasoning Addition
1 soup can water	½ cup cooked medium shell macaroni	¼ tsp. Louisiana-style hot sauce
1 soup can water	½ cup cubed cooked turkey *or* chicken	½ cup cooked mixed vegetables
1 soup can water	½ cup cooked elbow macaroni	½ cup cooked vegetable combination
1 soup can water	1 cup cubed cooked chicken	½ cup cooked whole kernel corn
1 soup can milk	1 cup cubed cooked chicken	½ cup cooked mixed vegetables

HEARTY VEGETABLE BEAN SOUP

2 tbsp. olive oil

2 large zucchini, cut in half lengthwise and sliced

¼ tsp. garlic powder

2 cans (10½ oz. *each*) CAMPBELL'S condensed Chicken Broth

1 soup can water

½ tsp. dried basil leaves, crushed

1 can (14½ oz.) whole peeled tomatoes, cut up

½ cup dry elbow twist *or* corkscrew macaroni

1 can (about 15 oz.) kidney beans, rinsed and drained

Grated Parmesan cheese

1 In saucepan over medium heat, heat oil. Cook zucchini and garlic powder until tender-crisp.

2 Add broth, water, basil and *undrained* tomatoes. Heat to a boil. Stir in macaroni. Cook over medium heat 10 min. or until macaroni is done, stirring occasionally.

3 Add beans. Heat through. Serve with cheese. If desired, garnish with *fresh basil*.

Makes 5 servings
Prep Time: 10 min.
Cook Time: 25 min.

VEGETABLE BEEF SOUP

2 cans (10½ oz. *each*) CAMPBELL'S condensed Beef Broth

2 cups water

¼ tsp. dried thyme leaves, crushed

⅛ tsp. pepper

1 medium potato, cut into cubes

1 bag (16 oz.) frozen mixed vegetables

½ cup cut-up canned tomatoes

1½ cups cubed cooked beef

In saucepan mix broth, water, thyme, pepper, potato, mixed vegetables and tomatoes. Over medium-high heat, heat to a boil. Cover and cook over low heat 15 min. or until vegetables are tender. Add beef. Heat through.

Makes 4 servings
Prep Time: 15 min.
Cook Time: 25 min.

MAKE IT HEARTY

Start with a can of soup and add a few simple ingredients. Try one of these souper-quick recipes to make mealtime delicious *and* easy! For more great recipes, just look at the back label on the can!

Pictured clockwise from top left: Hearty Noodle Soup, Hearty Old Fashioned Vegetable Soup and Hearty Beef Soup.

MAKE IT HEARTY:	CAMPBELL'S Soup
Hearty Noodle Soup	1 can (10¾ oz.) Chicken Noodle Soup
Hearty Old Fashioned Vegetable Soup	1 can (10½ oz.) Old Fashioned Vegetable Soup
Hearty Beef Soup	1 can (11 oz.) Beef Soup
Hearty Double Noodle Soup	1 can (11 oz.) DOUBLE NOODLE Soup
Hearty Green Pea Soup	1 can (11½ oz.) Green Pea Soup

METHOD: In saucepan, combine soup, water *or* milk and ADDITIONS.
Over medium heat, heat through, stirring often. Serves 2.

Water/Milk	Meat/Pasta Addition	Vegetable Addition
1 soup can water	½ cup cubed cooked chicken	½ cup cooked broccoli cuts
1 soup can water	1 cup cooked corkscrew macaroni	1 can (about 8 oz.) stewed tomatoes
1 soup can water	————————	½ cup cooked cut green beans ½ cup cooked whole kernel corn ½ cup cut-up canned tomatoes Generous dash pepper
1 soup can water	½ cup cubed cooked chicken	½ cup cooked whole kernel corn
1 soup can milk	1 cup cubed cooked ham	½ cup cooked sliced carrots

SOUPER SIDES & MORE

Tomato Zucchini Medley, left (page 57) and
Mushroom Broccoli Alfredo, right (page 56).

MUSHROOM BROCCOLI ALFREDO

2 tbsp. margarine
3 cups broccoli flowerets
3 cups sliced mushrooms
1 medium onion, coarsely chopped
¼ tsp. garlic powder
**1 can (10¾ oz.) CAMPBELL'S condensed
    Cream of Mushroom Soup**
⅓ cup milk
⅛ tsp. pepper
2 tbsp. grated Parmesan cheese
4 cups hot cooked fettuccine

1 In skillet over medium heat, heat margarine. Cook broccoli, mushrooms, onion and garlic powder until tender-crisp.

2 Add soup, milk, pepper and cheese. Heat through, stirring occasionally. Serve over fettuccine. If desired, garnish with *plum tomatoes, fresh oregano* and *fresh rosemary.*

Makes 4 servings
Prep Time: 15 min.
Cook Time: 15 min.

Select broccoli with compact clusters of tightly-closed flowerets that are dark-green, not yellowish. Avoid heads with broad, woody stems.

CREAMY VEGETABLE MEDLEY

**1 can (10¾ oz.) CAMPBELL'S condensed
    Cream of Celery Soup**
½ cup milk
2 cups broccoli flowerets
2 medium carrots, sliced
1 cup cauliflower flowerets

In saucepan mix soup, milk, broccoli, carrots and cauliflower. Over medium heat, heat to a boil. Cover and cook over low heat 15 min. or until vegetables are tender, stirring occasionally.

Makes 6 servings
Prep Time: 15 min.
Cook Time: 20 min.

TOMATO ZUCCHINI MEDLEY

1 can (10¾ oz.) CAMPBELL'S condensed
   Tomato Soup
1 tbsp. lemon juice
½ tsp. dried basil leaves, crushed
½ tsp. garlic powder
4 medium zucchini, sliced
1 small green pepper, cut into 2"-long strips
1 large onion, sliced
¼ cup grated Parmesan cheese

In Dutch oven mix soup, lemon juice, basil, garlic powder, zucchini, pepper and onion. Over medium heat, heat to a boil. Cover and cook over low heat 15 min. or until vegetables are tender, stirring occasionally. Stir in cheese. If desired, garnish with *additional Parmesan cheese.*

Makes 8 servings
Prep Time: 15 min.
Cook Time: 25 min.

When selecting fresh zucchini, look for tender, glossy skins free from bruises and blemishes. Choose zucchini that are slender in diameter and about 6" to 7" long.

GREEN BEAN BAKE

1 can (10¾ oz.) CAMPBELL'S condensed
   Cream of Mushroom Soup
½ cup milk
1 tsp. soy sauce
   Dash pepper
4 cups cooked cut green beans
1 can (2.8 oz.) French fried onions

1 In 1½-qt. casserole mix soup, milk, soy, pepper, beans and *½ can* onions.

2 Bake at 350°F. 25 min. or until hot.

3 Stir. Sprinkle remaining onions over top. Bake 5 min. or until onions are golden.

Makes 6 servings
Prep Time: 10 min.
Cook Time: 30 min.

BAKED MAC 'N' CHEESE

**2 cans (10¾ oz. *each*) CAMPBELL'S
    condensed Cheddar Cheese Soup**
1 soup can milk
¼ tsp. pepper
4 cups hot cooked corkscrew macaroni
2 tbsp. dry bread crumbs
1 tbsp. margarine, melted

1 In 2-qt. casserole mix soup, milk, pepper and macaroni.
2 Sprinkle bread crumbs mixed with margarine over top. Bake at 400°F. 25 min. or until hot. If desired, garnish with *carrot flowers* and *fresh mint*.

Makes 8 servings
Prep Time: 20 min.
Cook Time: 25 min.

**For 4 cups cooked corkscrew macaroni,
use 8 oz. or 3 cups dry.**

FIESTA TOMATO RICE

1 tbsp. vegetable oil
1 large onion, chopped
1 large green pepper, chopped
⅛ tsp. garlic powder
1 cup uncooked regular long-grain rice
**1 can (11⅛ oz.) CAMPBELL'S condensed
    Fiesta Tomato Soup**
2 cups water

1 In saucepan over medium heat, heat oil. Cook onion, pepper and garlic powder until tender-crisp.
2 Add rice and cook 30 sec., stirring constantly. Stir in soup and water. Heat to a boil. Cover and cook over low heat 25 min. or until rice is done.

Makes 4 servings
Prep Time: 10 min.
Cook Time: 35 min.

Vegetable Rotini

2½ cups dry corkscrew macaroni

1½ cups broccoli flowerets

1½ cups cauliflower flowerets

  2 medium carrots, cut into 2" matchstick-thin strips

  1 pkg. (3 oz.) cream cheese, softened

  1 can (10¾ oz.) CAMPBELL'S condensed Broccoli Cheese Soup

¾ cup milk

  2 tbsp. Dijon-style mustard (optional)

⅛ tsp. pepper

½ cup grated Parmesan cheese

1 In saucepan prepare macaroni according to pkg. directions. Add broccoli, cauliflower and carrots last 5 min. of cooking. Drain in colander.

2 In same pan stir cream cheese until smooth. Stir in soup, milk, mustard, pepper and Parmesan cheese. Over low heat, heat through. Add macaroni mixture. Heat through, stirring occasionally.

Makes 6 servings

Prep Time: 15 min.

Cook Time: 20 min.

To soften cream cheese, remove from wrapper. On microwave-safe plate, microwave on HIGH 10 sec.

Cheddar Potato Slices

  1 can (10¾ oz.) CAMPBELL'S condensed Cream of Mushroom Soup

½ tsp. paprika

½ tsp. pepper

  4 medium baking potatoes, sliced ¼" thick

  1 cup shredded Cheddar cheese

1 Mix soup, paprika and pepper. In greased 2-qt. shallow baking dish arrange potatoes in overlapping rows. Sprinkle with cheese. Spoon soup mixture over potatoes.

2 Cover and bake at 400°F. 45 min. Uncover and bake 10 min. or until potatoes are tender.

Makes 6 servings

Prep Time: 15 min.

Cook Time: 55 min.

SQUASH CASSEROLE

3 cups PEPPERIDGE FARM Corn Bread _or_ Herb Seasoned Stuffing
¼ cup margarine, melted
1 can (10¾ oz.) CAMPBELL'S condensed Cream of Chicken Soup
½ cup sour cream
½ cup shredded Cheddar cheese
2 small yellow squash, shredded
2 small zucchini, shredded
¼ cup shredded carrot

1 Mix stuffing and margarine. Reserve _½ cup_ stuffing mixture. Spread remaining stuffing mixture in 2-qt. shallow baking dish.

2 Mix soup, sour cream, cheese, yellow squash, zucchini and carrot. Spread soup mixture over stuffing mixture.

3 Sprinkle reserved stuffing mixture over top. Bake at 350°F. 40 min. or until hot.

Makes 8 servings
Prep Time: 15 min.
Cook Time: 40 min.

Whether it's green or yellow, squash will stay fresh for up to 5 days in the refrigerator if sealed tightly inside a plastic bag.

SOUPER-QUICK GUMBO RICE

1 can (10¾ oz.) CAMPBELL'S condensed Chicken Gumbo Soup
1 cup water
⅛ tsp. garlic powder
⅛ tsp. onion powder
1¼ cups uncooked instant rice

1 In saucepan mix soup, water, garlic powder and onion powder. Over medium-high heat, heat to a boil.

2 Stir in rice. Cover and set aside 5 min. Fluff with fork.

Makes 3 servings
Prep Time: 5 min.
Cook Time: 5 min.
Stand Time: 5 min.

SPEEDY
SAUCES &
SANDWICHES

Cheddar Cheese Sauce, left (page 66), Fiesta Tacos, center
(page 67) and Italian Potato Topper, right (page 66).

CHEDDAR CHEESE SAUCE

1 can (10¾ oz.) CAMPBELL'S condensed Cheddar Cheese Soup
⅓ cup milk

In saucepan mix soup and milk. Over low heat, heat through, stirring often. Serve over cooked broccoli, cauliflower, carrots, mixed vegetables, baked potatoes, French fries, omelets *or* pasta.

Makes 1½ cups
Prep Time: 5 min.
Cook Time: 5 min.

To bake four potatoes, pierce potatoes with fork. Bake at 400°F. 1 hr. or microwave on HIGH 10½ to 12½ min. *or* until fork-tender.

ITALIAN POTATO TOPPER

1 can (10¾ oz.) CAMPBELL'S condensed Cream of Mushroom Soup
Dash pepper
2 cups frozen Italian-style vegetable combination
¼ cup grated Parmesan cheese
4 hot baked potatoes, split
Chopped tomato

1 In saucepan mix soup, pepper, vegetables and cheese. Over medium heat, heat to a boil.
2 Cover and cook over low heat 5 min. or until vegetables are tender, stirring occasionally. Serve over potatoes. Top with tomato.

Makes 4 servings
Prep Time: 5 min.
Cook Time: 10 min.

Fiesta Tacos

1 lb. ground beef
1 can (11⅛ oz.) CAMPBELL'S condensed
    Fiesta Tomato Soup
8 taco shells
1 cup shredded lettuce
1 medium tomato, chopped
1 cup shredded Cheddar cheese

1 In skillet over medium-high heat, cook beef until browned, stirring to separate meat. Pour off fat.
2 Add soup. Over low heat, heat through. Divide meat mixture among taco shells. Top with lettuce, tomato and cheese.

Makes 8 tacos
Prep Time: 10 min.
Cook Time: 10 min.

Tangy Tomato Grilled Beef Sandwiches

1 can (10¾ oz.) CAMPBELL'S condensed
    Tomato Soup
2 tbsp. packed brown sugar
2 tbsp. lemon juice
2 tbsp. vegetable oil
1 tbsp. Worcestershire sauce
1 tsp. garlic powder
¼ tsp. dried thyme leaves, crushed
1½ lb. boneless beef sirloin steak, ¾" thick
6 round sandwich rolls, split

1 Mix soup, sugar, lemon juice, oil, Worcestershire, garlic powder and thyme.
2 Grill steak on lightly oiled grill rack over medium-hot coals to desired doneness (15 min. for medium), turning once and brushing often with soup mixture. Slice steak into thin strips.
3 Heat remaining soup mixture to a boil. Divide steak among 6 roll halves. Top with soup mixture and remaining roll halves.

Makes 6 sandwiches
Prep Time: 10 min.
Cook Time: 15 min.

ITALIAN BURGER MELT

1½ lb. ground beef
1 can (11⅛ oz.) CAMPBELL'S condensed Italian Tomato Soup
⅓ cup water
6 slices American cheese
6 hamburger rolls, split and toasted

1 Shape beef into 6 patties, ½" thick.
2 In skillet over medium-high heat, cook patties in 2 batches until browned. Set patties aside. Pour off fat.

3 Add soup and water. Heat to a boil. Return patties to pan. Cover and cook over low heat 10 min. or until patties are done (160°F.).
4 Place cheese on patties and cook until cheese is melted. Place patties on 6 roll halves. Top with soup mixture and remaining roll halves.

Makes 6 sandwiches
Prep Time: 10 min.
Cook Time: 30 min.

Beef 'n' Bean Burritos

1 lb. ground beef
1 small onion, chopped
1 can (11¼ oz.) CAMPBELL'S condensed
    Fiesta Chili Beef Soup
¼ cup water
8 flour tortillas (8")
    Shredded Cheddar cheese
    PACE Thick & Chunky Salsa
    Sour cream (optional)

1   In skillet over medium-high heat, cook beef and
    onion until beef is browned, stirring to separate meat.
    Pour off fat.

2   Add soup and water. Over low heat, heat through.

3   Warm tortillas according to pkg. directions. Spoon
    meat mixture down center of each tortilla. Top with
    cheese, salsa and sour cream. Fold tortilla around
    filling. If desired, garnish with *cherry tomatoes* and
    fresh parsley.

Makes 8 burritos
Prep Time: 10 min.
Cook Time: 10 min.

CHICKEN FAJITAS

¼ **cup prepared Italian salad dressing**
6 **skinless, boneless chicken breast halves**
1 **can (11 oz.) CAMPBELL'S condensed Fiesta Nacho Cheese Soup**
⅓ **cup milk**
12 **flour tortillas (6")**
4 **green onions, thinly sliced**
1 **small avocado, peeled, pitted and sliced (optional)**

1 Pour dressing into large shallow nonmetallic dish. Add chicken and turn to coat. Cover and refrigerate 30 min.

2 Remove chicken from marinade. Discard marinade. Grill chicken on lightly oiled grill rack over medium-hot coals 15 min. or until chicken is done, turning once.

3 In saucepan mix soup and milk. Over medium heat, heat through, stirring often.

4 Warm tortillas according to pkg. directions. Slice chicken into thin strips and place down center of each tortilla. Top with onions, avocado and soup mixture. Fold tortilla around filling. If desired, garnish with *assorted sweet peppers.*

Makes 12 fajitas
Prep Time: 5 min.
Marinating Time: 30 min.
Cook Time: 15 min.

CREAMY CHICKEN BROCCOLI SAUCE

1 **can (10¾ oz.) CAMPBELL'S condensed Cream of Chicken & Broccoli Soup**
½ **cup milk**
⅛ **tsp. pepper**

In saucepan mix soup, milk and pepper. Over medium heat, heat through, stirring often. Serve over grilled or broiled chicken, rice or noodles.

Makes about 1½ cups
Prep Time: 5 min.
Cook Time: 5 min.

SOUPERBURGER SANDWICHES

1 **lb. ground beef**
1 **medium onion, chopped**
1 **can (10¾ oz.) CAMPBELL'S condensed**
    Cream of Celery Soup
1 **tbsp. prepared mustard**
⅛ **tsp. pepper**
6 **round sandwich *or* hamburger rolls,**
    split and toasted

1 In skillet over medium-high heat, cook beef and
   onion until beef is browned, stirring to separate meat.
   Pour off fat.

2 Add soup, mustard and pepper. Over low heat, heat
   through. Divide meat mixture among 6 roll halves.
   Top with remaining roll halves.

Makes 6 sandwiches
Prep Time: 5 min.
Cook Time: 10 min.

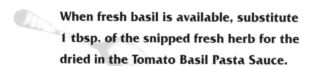

**When fresh basil is available, substitute
1 tbsp. of the snipped fresh herb for the
dried in the Tomato Basil Pasta Sauce.**

TOMATO BASIL PASTA SAUCE

1 **can (10¾ oz.) CAMPBELL'S condensed**
    Broccoli Cheese Soup
¾ **cup half-and-half *or* milk**
1 **tsp. dried basil leaves, crushed**
3 **plum tomatoes, coarsely chopped**
¼ **cup grated Parmesan cheese**
3 **cups hot cooked fettuccine**

In saucepan mix soup, half-and-half, basil, tomatoes
and cheese. Over medium heat, heat to a boil. Cook
over low heat 5 min., stirring occasionally. Toss with
fettuccine.

Makes about 2½ cups sauce *or* 4 servings
Prep Time: 10 min.
Cook Time: 10 min.

CHICKEN QUESADILLAS

1 can (10¾ oz.) CAMPBELL'S condensed
  Cream of Chicken Soup
1 jalapeño pepper, seeded and finely
  chopped (optional)
1 cup shredded Cheddar cheese
1½ cups chopped cooked chicken
8 flour tortillas (8")
  PACE Thick & Chunky Salsa
  Sour cream

1 Mix soup, pepper, ½ *cup* cheese and chicken.

2 Place tortillas on 2 baking sheets. Top half of each tortilla with ¼ *cup* soup mixture. Spread to within ½" of edge. Moisten edges of tortillas with water. Fold over and press edges together.

3 Bake at 400°F. 8 min. or until tortillas are crisp. Sprinkle with remaining cheese. Serve with salsa and sour cream.

Makes 4 servings
Prep Time: 15 min.
Cook Time: 8 min.

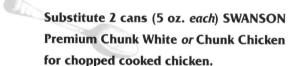

Substitute 2 cans (5 oz. *each*) SWANSON Premium Chunk White *or* Chunk Chicken for chopped cooked chicken.

HERB GRILLING SAUCE

1 can (10½ oz.) CAMPBELL'S condensed
  Chicken Broth
3 tbsp. lemon juice
1 tsp. dried basil leaves, crushed
1 tsp. dried thyme leaves, crushed
⅛ tsp. pepper

Mix broth, lemon juice, basil, thyme and pepper. Use to baste chicken, fish or pork during grilling or broiling.

Makes about 1 cup
Prep Time: 5 min.

Chicken Quesadillas

BROCCOLI CHEESE POTATO TOPPER

1 **can (10¾ oz.) CAMPBELL'S condensed Cheddar Cheese Soup**

2 **tbsp. sour cream**

½ **tsp. Dijon-style mustard**

1 **cup cooked broccoli flowerets**

4 **hot baked potatoes, split**

1 In saucepan mix soup, sour cream, mustard and broccoli. Over medium heat, heat through, stirring occasionally.

2 Serve over potatoes. If desired, garnish with *chopped sweet red pepper.*

Makes 4 servings

Prep Time: 10 min.

Cook Time: 10 min.

BEEF-TOPPED POTATOES

1 **can (19 oz.) CAMPBELL'S CHUNKY Beef Soup**

⅛ **tsp. pepper**

1 **cup cooked broccoli flowerets**

3 **hot baked potatoes, split**

Shredded Cheddar cheese

1 In saucepan mix soup, pepper and broccoli. Over medium heat, heat through, stirring occasionally.

2 Serve over potatoes. Top with cheese.

Makes 3 servings

Prep Time: 10 min.

Cook Time: 5 min.

FIESTA CHILI BEEF POTATO TOPPER

1 **lb. ground beef**

1 **small green pepper, chopped**

1 **small onion, chopped**

1 **can (11¼ oz.) CAMPBELL'S condensed Fiesta Chili Beef Soup**

1 **can (14½ oz.) whole peeled tomatoes, cut up**

4 **hot baked potatoes, split**

Shredded Cheddar cheese

1 In skillet over medium-high heat, cook beef, pepper and onion until beef is browned, stirring to separate meat. Pour off fat.

2 Add soup and *undrained* tomatoes. Over low heat, heat through.

3 Serve over potatoes. Top with cheese.

Makes 4 servings

Prep Time: 10 min.

Cook Time: 15 min.

There's no quicker way to cook potatoes than in the microwave. Scrub the potato skin with a vegetable brush, pierce with a fork and microwave on HIGH for 3 to 5 min. per spud. Rearrange potatoes once during cooking.

Clockwise from top left: Fiesta Chili Beef Potato Topper, Broccoli Cheese Potato Topper and Beef-Topped Potatoes.

No-Fuss
Nibbles

Clockwise from left: Vegetable Quesadillas (page 81),
Tex-Mex Dip (page 81) and Souper Mushroom Pizza (page 80).

SOUPER MUSHROOM PIZZA

1 loaf (about 1 lb.) Italian bread (16" long),
    cut in half lengthwise
1 can (10¾ oz.) CAMPBELL'S condensed
    Cream of Mushroom Soup
¼ tsp. garlic powder
¼ tsp. Italian seasoning, crushed
1 cup shredded mozzarella cheese
1 tbsp. grated Parmesan cheese
1 small green *or* sweet red pepper, chopped
2 green onions, chopped

1 Bake bread on baking sheet at 400°F. 5 min. or until lightly toasted.

2 Mix soup, garlic powder and Italian seasoning. Stir in mozzarella cheese, Parmesan cheese, pepper and onions.

3 Spread soup mixture on bread. Bake 5 min. or until cheese is melted. Cut each bread half into 12 slices. If desired, garnish with *fresh oregano* and *additional sweet red pepper.*

Makes 24 appetizers
Prep Time: 15 min.
Cook Time: 5 min.

PARTY MEATBALLS

1 can (11⅛ oz.) CAMPBELL'S condensed
    Italian Tomato Soup
1 lb. ground beef
¼ cup dry bread crumbs
1 egg, beaten
1 tbsp. Worcestershire sauce
½ cup water
2 tbsp. vinegar
2 tsp. packed brown sugar

1 Mix *¼ cup* soup, beef, bread crumbs, egg and Worcestershire *thoroughly* and shape *firmly* into 48 (½") meatballs. Arrange in shallow-sided baking pan.

2 Bake at 350°F. 15 min. or until meatballs are done.

3 In saucepan mix remaining soup, water, vinegar and sugar. Over medium heat, heat to a boil. Cover and cook over low heat 5 min. Add meatballs. Heat through.

Makes 48 appetizers
Prep Time: 20 min.
Cook Time: 30 min.

TEX-MEX DIP

1 can (11¼ oz.) CAMPBELL'S condensed
    Fiesta Chili Beef Soup
⅓ cup **OPEN PIT Original Flavor Barbecue**
    Sauce
2 tbsp. **finely chopped green pepper**
1 tbsp. **finely chopped onion**
    Sour cream
    Tortilla chips

In saucepan mix soup, barbecue sauce, pepper and onion. Over medium heat, heat through, stirring often. Top with sour cream. Serve with tortilla chips for dipping. If desired, garnish with *fresh chives* and *chili peppers.*

Makes 1½ cups
Prep Time: 10 min.
Cook Time: 5 min.

Wear rubber gloves to protect your hands from the burning oils when handling and seeding jalapeño peppers.

VEGETABLE QUESADILLAS

1 can (10¾ oz.) **CAMPBELL'S condensed**
    Cheddar Cheese Soup
¼ cup **milk**
1 medium **tomato, chopped**
1 medium **green pepper, chopped**
2 **green onions, sliced**
1 **jalapeño pepper, seeded and finely**
    chopped (optional)
6 **flour tortillas (6")**
    PACE Thick & Chunky Salsa
    Sour cream

1 Mix soup, milk, tomato, green pepper, onions and jalapeño pepper.

2 Place tortillas on 2 baking sheets. Top each tortilla with about *⅓ cup* soup mixture. Spread to within ½" of edge.

3 Bake at 400°F. 10 min. or until tortillas are crisp. Cut each tortilla into quarters. Serve with salsa and sour cream.

Makes 24 appetizers
Prep Time: 15 min.
Cook Time: 10 min.

NACHOS

1 can (10¾ oz.) CAMPBELL'S condensed
   Cheddar Cheese Soup
½ cup PACE Thick & Chunky Salsa
1 bag (about 10 oz.) tortilla chips
   Chopped tomato
   Sliced green onions
   Sliced VLASIC *or* EARLY CALIFORNIA
     pitted Ripe Olives
   Chopped green *or* sweet red pepper

1 In saucepan mix soup and salsa. Over low heat, heat through, stirring often.
2 Serve over tortilla chips. Top with tomato, onions, olives and pepper.

Makes 6 appetizer servings
Prep Time: 10 min.
Cook Time: 5 min.

NACHOS GRANDE

1 can (11 oz.) CAMPBELL'S condensed
   Fiesta Nacho Cheese Soup
⅓ cup milk
1 lb. ground beef
1 small onion, chopped
5 cups tortilla chips (about 5 oz.)
1 medium tomato, chopped
1 jalapeño pepper, seeded and sliced
   (optional)

1 In saucepan mix soup and milk. Set aside.
2 In skillet over medium-high heat, cook beef and onion until beef is browned, stirring to separate meat. Pour off fat. Add ½ *cup* soup mixture. Over low heat, heat through.
3 Over medium heat, heat remaining soup mixture, stirring often.
4 Arrange chips on platter. Top with meat mixture. Spoon soup mixture over meat. Top with tomato and pepper.

Makes 8 appetizer servings
Prep Time: 10 min.
Cook Time: 10 min.

Tortilla Vegetable Bites

1 **pkg. (8 oz.) cream cheese, softened**
1 **pouch CAMPBELL'S Dry Onion Soup and Recipe Mix**
1 **tsp. Louisiana-style hot sauce**
1 **small carrot, shredded**
2 **green onions, chopped**
6 **flour tortillas (8")**

1 Stir cheese until smooth. Stir in soup mix, hot sauce, carrot and onions. Top each tortilla with about $1/4$ *cup* cheese mixture. Spread to edge. Tightly roll up like a jelly roll. Place seam-side down in shallow dish. Cover and refrigerate at least 2 hr.

2 Cut each roll-up into 1" slices. If desired, garnish with *jalapeño peppers, carrots* and *green onions*.

Makes 36 appetizers
Prep Time: 15 min.
Chill Time: 2 hr.

To soften cream cheese, remove from wrapper. On microwave-safe plate, microwave on HIGH 15 sec.

Onion Chicken Nuggets

1 **pouch CAMPBELL'S Dry Onion Soup and Recipe Mix**
$2/3$ **cup dry bread crumbs**
$1/8$ **tsp. pepper**
1 **egg**
2 **tbsp. water**
$1\frac{1}{2}$ **lb. skinless, boneless chicken, cut into 1" pieces**
2 **tbsp. margarine, melted (optional)**

1 Crush soup mix in pouch with rolling pin. Mix soup mix, bread crumbs and pepper on plate.

2 Mix egg and water in dish. Dip chicken into egg mixture. Coat with crumb mixture.

3 Place chicken on baking sheet. Drizzle with margarine. Bake at 400°F. 15 min. or until chicken is done.

Makes 10 appetizer servings
Prep Time: 20 min.
Cook Time: 15 min.

MEXICALI DIP

1 can (11½ oz.) CAMPBELL'S condensed
   Bean with Bacon Soup
½ cup sour cream
1 tsp. chili powder
½ cup PACE Thick & Chunky Salsa
1 cup shredded Cheddar cheese
   Sliced green onions
   Sliced VLASIC *or* EARLY CALIFORNIA
   pitted Ripe Olives
   Tortilla chips

Mix soup, sour cream and chili powder. Spread on 10" plate. Top with salsa, cheese, onions and olives. Serve with tortilla chips for dipping. If desired, garnish with *lemon* and *fresh parsley*.

Makes 1½ cups
Prep Time: 15 min.

To serve Mexicali Dip warm, use 10" microwave-safe plate and microwave on HIGH 2 min.

HONEY MUSTARD WINGS

1 pouch CAMPBELL'S Dry Onion Soup and
   Recipe Mix
⅓ cup honey
2 tbsp. spicy-brown mustard
18 chicken wings

1 Mix soup mix, honey and mustard. Set aside.
2 Cut wings at joints. Discard tips. In bowl toss wings with sauce.
3 Bake chicken in shallow-sided baking pan at 400°F. 45 min. or until chicken is done, turning once.

Makes 36 appetizers
Prep Time: 15 min.
Cook Time: 45 min.

Mexicali Dip

CINNAMON RAISIN LOAVES

Vegetable cooking spray
3 cups all-purpose flour
2 tsp. ground cinnamon
1 tsp. baking soda
½ tsp. baking powder
1½ cups sugar
1 can (10¾ oz.) CAMPBELL'S HEALTHY
    REQUEST condensed Tomato Soup
6 egg whites
⅓ cup vegetable oil
1 tsp. vanilla extract
2 cups shredded zucchini
1 cup raisins

1 Preheat oven to 350°F. Spray two 8½" x 4½" loaf pans with cooking spray. Set aside.

2 Mix flour, cinnamon, baking soda and baking powder. Set aside.

3 Mix sugar, soup, egg whites, oil and vanilla. Add to flour mixture, stirring just to moisten. Fold in zucchini and raisins. Pour into prepared pans.

4 Bake 55 min. or until toothpick inserted in center comes out clean. Cool in pans on wire rack 10 min. Remove from pans and cool on rack.

Makes 2 loaves (12 servings *each*)
Prep Time: 20 min.
Cook Time: 55 min.

SPINACH ALMOND DIP

1 pouch CAMPBELL'S Dry Onion Soup and
    Recipe Mix
1 container (16 oz.) sour cream
1 pkg. (about 10 oz.) frozen chopped
    spinach, thawed and well drained
⅓ cup chopped toasted almonds
    Chopped sweet red pepper
    Assorted crackers

Mix soup mix, sour cream, spinach and almonds. Refrigerate at least 2 hr. Top with pepper. Serve with crackers for dipping.

Makes 2½ cups
Prep Time: 10 min.
Chill Time: 2 hr.

TOMATO SOUP-SPICE CAKE

2 cups all-purpose flour
1⅓ cups sugar
4 tsp. baking powder
1½ tsp. ground allspice
1 tsp. baking soda
1 tsp. ground cinnamon
½ tsp. ground cloves
1 can (10¾ oz.) CAMPBELL'S condensed Tomato Soup
½ cup vegetable shortening
2 eggs
¼ cup water
Cream Cheese Frosting (recipe follows)

1 Preheat oven to 350°F. Grease and lightly flour 13" x 9" baking pan. Set aside.

2 Mix flour, sugar, baking powder, allspice, baking soda, cinnamon and cloves. Add soup, shortening, eggs and water. With mixer at low speed, beat until well mixed, constantly scraping bowl. At high speed, beat 4 min., occasionally scraping bowl. Pour into prepared pan.

3 Bake 40 min. or until toothpick inserted in center comes out clean. Cool in pan on wire rack 10 min. Remove from pan and cool on rack. Frost with Cream Cheese Frosting. If desired, garnish with *candied orange peel, cinnamon* and *edible flowers.*

Cream Cheese Frosting

In bowl with mixer at medium speed, beat 1 pkg. (8 oz.) cream cheese, softened; 2 tbsp. milk and 1 tsp. vanilla extract until creamy. Gradually beat in 1 pkg. (16 oz.) confectioners' sugar until smooth. Makes 3 cups.

Makes 12 servings
Prep Time: 20 min.
Cook Time: 40 min.
Cool Time: 30 min.

To retain their flavor and quality, it's a good idea to store dried spices away from direct sunlight and also in airtight containers, as moisture can cause spices to cake.

Tomato Soup-Spice Cake

RECIPE INDEX

RECIPE INDEX (CONT)

RECIPE INDEX (CONT)

RECIPES BY PRODUCT INDEX

RECIPES BY PRODUCT INDEX (CONT.)

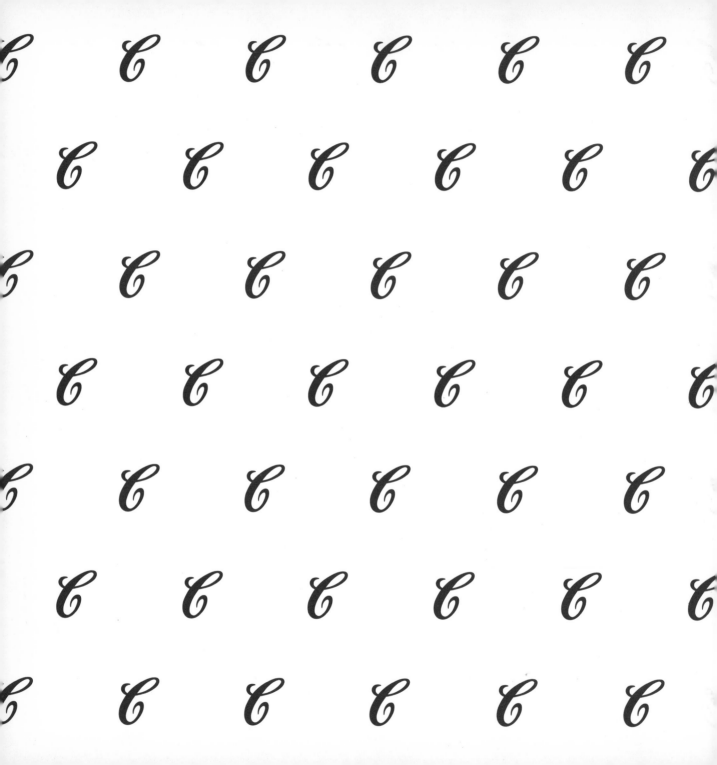